Blood Child

Blood Child

Eleanor Rees

First published 2015 by
Liverpool University Press
4 Cambridge Street
Liverpool
L69 7ZU

British Library Cataloguing-in-Publication data
A British Library CIP record is available

ISBN 978-1-78138-180-9 softback

Typeset by Carnegie Book Production, Lancaster
Printed and bound by Booksfactory.co.uk

We ... must recognise in the power of the imagination
the creative impulse of life itself in continually bringing forth
the forms we encounter, whether in art, through reading,
writing or painting, or in nature, through
walking in the landscape.

Tim Ingold

Rocks and winds, germs and words, are all different manifesta-
tions of this dynamic material reality ...
they all represent the different ways in which single
matter-energy expresses itself.

Manuel De Landa

Contents

A Burial of Sight

After 'Esmedune' by Adrian Henri

Sometimes there is another city,
    light and wide,
        shifting on continental plates –
          or icebergs,
            islands,
      ships that spread
        air around
          the building's substance,
        or pulled apart on rails, splayed out
as you travel
to the other boundary
and take a little of my sight.

I see the journey
      through the taxi window,
    how trees are a rich-green-rustling,
        your wide eyes
          casting a light
and I, strolling, somnolent,
      downhill towards a subtle river
        know the lighthouse downstream shimmers
          in sun-brown dusk,
        a flock of terns on the river's pull
        far from here, far over –
          sea wind an opening
          as I drop back into the city.
I tread on time.
I stand on its back and breathe.

*

Far rush of traffic,
      an in-breath, an out-breath.
           Stream, steady, full.

Bass notes, starlings,
a rustling car on the main road.

Clack of heels on hard tarmac.
Gulls gather on windowsills.

This time of day is a slip of a girl
      who carries night in her handbag,
      who lets it fall
           black spilling
      down side streets
darkening roofs
of the dusk-flooded town.

To the west sun is setting,
sinking with me into dark:

until when you emerge from the lake,
      a shimmer of gold at your eye's cusp.
         In the folds of the lid
      a speckle of heaven.

It skins you, this liquid,
         pulls down your edges,
    eyes shining like a buzzard's
      eyes in a moment of flight.

Love, here's a warm evening.
      We are above and over,
    skimming treetops,
      hovering like dragon flies.
         Our wings also gold and turquoise.

The lake rich with sludge
smells of bone meal.

You watch me dip my toes in,
unzip my skirt, slip
down into thick, brown water.

My skin is heavy with moisture,
pricked with heat.

I eat at mud with my tongue.
Mineral rich salt

drips from my skin
puddling and slithery.

There you are on shore,
walking away into dusk.

A heavy orange heat clutches
            earth with hot hands,
                  tilts his turning slightly,
            like a snow globe.
            I am hot and cold,
            made of mud so
            otherly, otherly.

*

In the woods beneath pine trees' green,
in shade, amongst the grasses,
rusty heat of the new dark
presses hard on my shoulders.

I am edges of indigo,
in this evening at the edge of time,
in the centre of the city.
It is my country.
Here in a settled centre of air

that busies gently at leaves'
flat veins,
wide-open palms
submitting to the sun.

I breathe the bright of turning dusk.
The openness reaches in;
air fills my lungs. I stretch and yawn.
The light is immediate.
The light is above, within.
It streams, a settling
of time in bone.

The shade around my feet
is loose and sandy.
I sink my toes into grains of light

and meld place to place.
I am shadow.
It is my skin.
I give way to shade and dusk.
Thought is too hard, too dominant.

What does silence mean?

I fall away from it and into brine,
into saliva's salt, sweet and warm.

The silence means sun is asleep
and waiting gently for the dawn.
He takes her home,
holds her warm.

She was the colour of winter.
His arms remake her heat.

There is another man that runs
out of breath through the morning streets

to love her, but is made of air.

He hits a wall like a ghost.

He loves only the invisible
world. In the day his

hands settle into stone
and thread straight through

glass, he bleeds
but only rain and air,

the morning dew –

then

this evening cool.

*

The light begins to crack.
Couples appear along the path
entering into felted green.

The coolness taps at my skin –
midges, a cough,
boys playing football cry and grunt.

Ducks in threes, a male and two females
waddle over tarmac,
orange feet on grey-black.
She dips her head into green-grass-verge,
settles in an oval, wobbles,
waits it seems –
though for who or why I can't say.

Consciousness is a sharp bite: a hailstorm.

I slip away from myself.

In the distance, weight
of Calder Stones

marks earth.
A love bite
roughed from a mountain's mouth.
Teeth of gods
bite up at the air.
He never leaves. Stone
is bound
and only disappears
in eroded glances
eyelash flashes or rain
across a wet cool back.

Stone man, hard and persistent,
I carved you up, gave your eyes.

The grey sky today has a film
of light behind thick cloud.

There's warmth behind this skin.

In the stone circle
is density and crushed atoms.

I dig for your roots so deeply held

and turn you over, flip back the light,
expose new day in its red raw,

skinless –

*

I am digging up the grasses,
              spading up the dirt,
        tipping up the ends,
                    worms and mineral gems.
They glitter in the sun –
are eyes, a burial of sight.

What does it look like underneath?

It looks like night.
Pinpricks of light filter through churned soil.
Stars? Yes but also fires
  on a plain, a valley of houses
      low in mist
  beneath a heavy winter browning light.

From above this soil
  is a meal, edible,
    a mouthful, but within it
  a toss and turn, covered
    with grit, a breath of salt
      in a bath of soil.

I bathe in earth,
  arms like moles plough tunnels into chalk.
Below here the light
  gurgles and deepens,
    pigments my skin with each splash and stroke.

I am buried,
  swimming beneath watercourse
      and tree root,
    crawling I suppose
  but with the freedom of worms.
The roots are lightning.
An underground stream speaks in swollen rushes.

My ears grasp onto sound
  and remember warm land
    above, where lovers
      are buckling in long grass,
    feet tread on the carpet
  as I am basemented,
    fallow and submerged
      in a well of substance.

Why does the substance never give way?

It does in a dream-fall,
a plummet from sky height,
the flight paths of geese above a city park.
In the night I am with them,
solid wings slapping against air currents,
almost like thoughts,
electrical pulses in my dream-soaked brain,
sodden with rest, dreary with a chemical
brew of darkness.

In here I fly, big-handed and huge,
big-flooded and balmy,
through the circumference of the park,
through wide blue reaches,
my goose-flesh heated and steady,
my feathers a sheen of dusk-light,
brown and white and black.
I skim you. I steal your dreams
and the Welsh hills beyond your valleys.
I swallow them into the beat of my wings,
into volley, puck and point,
a transition from north to south.
I fold you into a barrow of air,
bucketing within my wings to bask
at moon-height, the landscape
swelling like caught fish in a basket,
in the crook of my wings' ligament.
I hold it all here,
a haul of vision, all made substance
held close to me, warm and nested
in the hook of my goose heart.

Hot goose heart.

Hot goose beak.

I'll burrow for you.

Blood Child

Behind the house a single stark tree,
cherries still ripe though it is mid-winter.
Bletched fruit on bare branches ooze like a cut thumb,
each drop in slow motion falling onto hard soil.
Inside in a silent kitchen, on a metal table, apples curdle
in a handmade bowl; mulched bills ferment on varnished pine.
In the garden, past the pond, the tree stretches
like spilt ink, over-tall, bent back,
to eye a yellow crescent crisp in a fold of cloud.
Black night glass reflects back the dead centre of a pupil.

Blood drips from the mouth of the house.
Blood floods the dry seas of the moon.

On the stained-glass window of the empty hall
red flecks fall, become ice as hail chimes angular
to grey pebble-dash and dripping blood begins to take a form:
of a red-ice-child-creature, gleaming like a ruby
standing silent at the wind-opened door.
The storm glowers behind the outline like a tiger.
It roars but she cannot hear him.
You are not there to listen for her.
The hallway is an empty blue. Books rattle in their case.
Outside she stands like death. The door closes in her face.

Blood drips from the mouth of the house.
Blood floods the dry seas of the moon.

Where are you? Are you asleep in bed upstairs
or running breathless down the street?
Maybe you don't live here anymore?

Are you away in a cottage in the woods
or on a moving train, window patch-black smacked with yellow?
Are you underwater, swimming through
the last swathe of the tide? Are you listening for wolves
at the back of your mind? Are you in a hospital
deep under sterile silver and nurses' blue?
Yes, where are you?

Blood drips from the mouth of the house.
Blood floods the dry seas of the moon.

O Mother has gone missing, she has gone to ground
I sing abandoned at the outskirts of the town.

O Mother has gone missing, she has gone to ground
I sing as wolves' prowl around.

O Mother has gone missing, she has gone to ground
I sing a shining knife in hand.

O Mother has gone missing, she has gone to ground
I sing full-voiced with the choir of the land.

Yes, where are you?

In the garden, the tree flinches, scratched by rats,
the storm sifted from the watercourse;
small muscular movements smatter on a shield of dark.
Cherries gone, turned to child,
who crouches on the front step, red-ice-storm-creature
as bloodied as prey, silent as an unknown song,
as the snow comes along, the tree sighs and bows
and stretches again, under-tall, copying the hill, bends down.
In the house, on the living room floor, a wool rug
turns to water, small boats sail to wind-fed shores.

Blood drips from the mouth of the house.
Blood floods from the dry seas of the moon.

Are you underground, in the cellar or soil,
hiding in the mulch and leaves? Are you rooted
in the dirt or rolled up in the rot,
heart beating slow, lost light in your eye?
Or are you in the wood pile, kneeling under last year's pine
needles sticking into folded skin, or are you
gone from here, aloof in the wind like a wild goose
journeying south from darkness, garden soil
untended, land unturned? Are you un-become,
laid bare in the last light of winter sun?

Blood drips from the mouth of the house.
Blood floods the dry seas of the moon.

In the kitchen the tap drips a slow, red drop
onto stainless steel clouded with washing-up sods.
White light filters in through an open window.
Outside the garden heaves in wind; one breath.
A figure runs along the alley, a child or fox
but closer, starry red, her bright face at the glass.
The tree paws the soil like a horse, a branch
turning over loose earth with a sway, a lilt, a whip,
a crack but only as far as its roots will allow.
What is the spell that holds them still?

Blood drips from the mouth of the house.
Blood floods the dry seas of the moon.

It is the spell of silence,
child, she doesn't speak to the house.

It is the spell of silence,
child, she doesn't breathe to the frost.

It is the spell of silence,
child, she doesn't sound in her throat.

It is the spell of silence,
child, so she doesn't feel the loss.

Yes, where are you?

And the rats run to the river and the dogs
run to the river and the chimneys spark like kindling.
From far west flickers a firestorm through the town,
soot and smoke, sea buckling in distance,
a hot avalanche across frost-crested rooftops.
The red-ice-blood-creature waits on the doorstep,
listens for a high-pitched wail from the garden;
fat of a song. The tree is whipping hard
against the fence. It cannot run. Branches
stacked one-on-one form a shield. The fire comes.

Blood drips from the mouth of the house.
Blood floods the dry seas of the moon.

The house raises its head, tips back its neck.
In the hall a vase falls south; a ship in a storm.
Empty glasses smash their silence inside the kitchen cabinets.
A knitted doll tumbles down stripped wood stairs.
And underneath in foundations bricks
plough down into sandy earth like a rudder
and the bow of the building turns for the river.
The roof flips like a flag and the whole house
dredges through the molten earth which parts
like waves, splitting the garden wall, tarmac road.
Inside the schism, tree roots hang like curls.

Blood drips from the mouth of the house.
Blood floods the dry seas of the moon.

In the wall of mud, each frond turn, forms
a human face, oval-shaped, which calls out, *Where are you?*
Fire on the horizon crumples church-towers
as the red-ice-blood-creature starts to drip and ooze,
a snowman after snow has gone, warmth
scythes the sides of her small girl shape and becomes
a spring, a stream, a brook, a tidal river shifting mud
and roots to form a gorge with wooded sides;
through leaves two figures run, girl and woman,
each a ruby mark amongst a basalt green.

Blood drips from the mouth of the house.
Blood floods the dry seas of the moon.

And their melting blood flattens the fire.
At the crest of the ridge, as large as the sun,
lamp-lit town below like embers in the hearth,
steam in the street now quiet as cold the woman
who was a tree reaches out a hand to catch a crescent
painted onto navy cloth, tilts it back and forth,
then picks up her child, the red-ice-blood-creature
and pours her like lava onto the crust of the moon,
staining it sticky and the light spills like wine over the valley,
and a single cherry tree, in a garden, behind an empty house,
the fruit still ripe though it is mid-winter.

Blood drips from the mouth of the house.
Blood floods the dry seas of the moon.

Full

Moon-raked, unable to sleep,
I wake landlocked
and unwilling to shift beyond
my own horizon
into a fall of snow, or a tired
embrace, or a landscape
of ships and sails, old relics
on the shore, or your hand
again or the draw and wreck
of the sea on coastal plains
that is lapping even now:
2.35 a.m. late, unearthed
and deep in a city's sleepy silence
that's remarkable and unsung,
no trains, no rush of cars;
just this flat moment
heavy in the black cloudless sky.

The church on the hill
squats in a square of shadow
under the moon-ridden moments
of shifting white, and somewhere
inside perhaps near the altar
or in the pews she is sitting
alert to our dreams, hat on
for Sunday, hunched forward
in prayer. The door creaks
as I enter, sleep-frenzied
and aware of the turn of her neck:
her startled eyes
in the shadows witness
my night-time intrusion
into the life of the dark.

Tide

Behind the railway cutting
curtained windows are still drawn tight.
Aerial masts on newly-tiled roofs
point east: a train from Manchester
scowls west further into
the lock of houses, over the bridge
to the scraps of hedges where the foxes
live border-crossing the line
at dusk to the Mystery and the school car park;
and always down towards the sea
that is pulling all movement out with its
back arched, the landscape on ropes,
the city afloat, dragging all to the horizon:
water at our knees, gulls on the bow.

Mainline Rail

Back-to-backs, some of the last,
and always just below the view

a sunken tide of regular sound
west to the river, south to elsewhere;

and sometimes we travel together
as I slink into their sleep whilst I sleep,

settle beside a mother with a child
coiled in her lap, click-clacking

into darkness, coming heavy,
pushing at the edges of the carriage.

And sometimes the track returns us
on the late train to the end of my bed,

luggage in one hand, my jumper in another
until they fling themselves

out of the open window,

flit though ivy, nettles and wire
to meet the fast train home,

waking in a stuffy carriage,
an image of my room in their eye,

the tone of the city in their ear,
in the thrust of the train's rush

towards the sea and out of here.

Dusk Town

Shadow from the bridge slips through curtained windows
of an upstairs bedroom of a terraced house,
shifts across the duvet of a sleeping child
dreaming of the sun, as rain begins again
bustling through clouds like shoppers on Church Street.

In the music store a guitarist thumbs a chord
calling the clouds from cooling towers down river.

A young man who drowned in 1815 rises up and walks
towards his home on Mersey Road.
Water drips from his old bones. As he knocks
the door opens to the fire and a hunk of bread.

Bells ring; the transporter bridge swings towards Widnes.
Boys hang from steel girders, drop into high waters;
a jet plane slices the sky from east to west,
rain tacks to winds from distant seas up stream.

Across Castle Hill, a woman rides a horse into her fort,
woven mantle wet with sweat, a broth in the pot,
as atop the new steelwork of Jubilee Bridge
a welder jumps the final gap to be the first to cross,
legs stretched in mid-air above a rising tide.

Runcorn shakes itself down, dusts off fine drizzle;
gulls scatter. In the close-built Old Town streets
children carry church banners on the Whit parade,
molten tarmac sticks to their shoes in midday sun.
Over in the New Town a young couple come from the city
watch the light shift through an oval window.

A teenage boy kisses a pink-haired girl by the library,
as out where the waters widen

the drill bit burrows into the sandstone grit
testing for the foundations of an un-built bridge,
seen only in the gull's eyes it flips like a fish.

In the pub an old sailor lifts a fork on a plate of chips,
smiles as shadows sail along the High Street.
A mermaid, lost inland, sculls through dark alleys,
her tail reflects back the full moon
and the curve of the earth. She dives.

Arne's Progress

Crossing Over

As he sails the coracle of willow and skins,
his bird eyes mirror the moon behind cloud.
Spring tide drags west but he paddles east.
Water seeps through the stitching a little like blood.
Arne buckles his weight over the hump of the river,
the small craft alive on the back of the wave
as he waits for the hook to reveal his possessions:
pot of ink, hunk of amethyst, a drawing
of a storm framed in gold and made of light.

He wraps these in hessian, a swaddle of ornament,
pulls up a line as the clouds move south,
rain simpers along the Welsh mountains,
calling 'Go home now. Find a dent
in the earth and burrow in'. He sings
to the wind, rows the harrying waters.
Across the estuary a ship bell starts to ring.

An Irish ferry slows its entry into the detritus
of objects on the river awaiting the storm:
a broken slate, rat's corpse, torn lace, a mirror,
the thought of the future in a golden case
open to spray, velvet inlay sodden with salt.
A handful of red hair floats like a jelly fish
caught in the to-and-fro, in the froth of the drag.
A cormorant extends its shining black feathers
as he walks ashore on the bone of the wing.

St. James's Infirmary

In the graveyard the children have cholera.
They lie on stretchers, on iron-framed hospital beds.
He is mopping their foreheads with mildew,
parchment, moss, quietness and winter rain

which he did until just before dawn;
long hours of talk, laughter, occasional song.
The light from the moon made everything white.

He gave them gifts of fresh river water
and they drank with their mouths as silent as stars,
small hands cupped around the tankard,
milk teeth tapping on the cold edge of copper.

Philharmonic

Arne listens to lager fizz in long glasses
and talk of staying out all night.

Tomorrow will be sleeping in,
hot breath, sweat, some slow love
amongst well-worn sheets.

But tonight under the chandeliers,
tiled walls, silted green, a haul of banter
caught at 5.30; the river's tide still high,

a violinist plays Dvořák in the shadows
as the bargirl takes his order in Irish.

Cortège

With reins folded under his third finger and thumb,
black horses high-step oiled hooves,
feathered plumes braided to their bridles.

The avenue pulses and flames, and windows smash.
A lad struggles forward, head bloodied.
A police van screeches round the corner out of view.
The horses do not bolt or flinch but hold their heads up high
as a parked car ignites and burns out in a breath.

Arne gathers the embers and tar into a jar.
The ashes he places in the back of the hearse.
Spring flowers entwine SISTER along the coffin lid

and on he drives as lamp-posts scale back
from sodium to oil, and a setting sun dampens the fires.

A bulldozer gouges an end terrace's eyes,
as an old woman in her kitchen watches through the window,
a cup of tea in her shaking hands,

and on he drives over cherry blossoms splattered on tarmac
while a man at the bus stop scrambles through a sandstorm
to a hut in the village where a brother was murdered.

At the traffic lights an 80A pounces from the junction
and ploughs straight through the oncoming hearse,
his horses enjoying the sensation of diesel,

sweat and steam in their bellies, in their long flowing manes.
They emerge on the other side
still composed, still clattering home.

Sheen

A seagull is flapping its wings in the glasshouse
as Arne stares in, globe-faced and shining,
at tables laid for dinner under the height of the palms;

and as the bird rises the vaulted roof blossoms
then derelict again, window frames reveal grey clouds
to wedding guests observing the gull's flight into time.

Yet the marriage is still perfect, transparent and glowing.
A spun-silk bride, a cake opaque as ice,
a slow first dance amongst the exotic plants.

And as he watches the glass house spin on its axis,
marble botanists in the garden slowing the sway
while white doors break open, cough jasmine pink petals.

Arne walks among the scent of salt and manure.
Heat sweats his vision, colour drips to the floor.

Magnolia

Arne lies watching shadows
waft across wallpaper,

hands behind his head, toes to the ceiling,
on the slightly-soiled white sheets

until he begins to seep again.
A draft blows through the corridor,

catches, and he is away into the brickwork,
mouthful of mortar and plaster

in his stomach's translucent core,
a bright sack of minerals digesting into dust;

and then he is on the decking, waiting,
while rain drips through his contours

as he lounges on the garden furniture;
rotten wood swollen with fungi.

The parkland beyond the trellis
brims with water;

a woman with a pushchair
runs into a shelter.

He pours into the rain, holds her hand.
Lets her breathe.

Becoming Miniature

Red twigs jut into the space, into the August sun. Grey
under ivy tendril spills a stillness. Spluttering gusts.

The metal roof of the parked car sparks. Slate tiles beyond
the stretch of garden wall are circled by a bird that flies in a loop

and away behind the houses pressed with satellite dishes.
Aerials all point west as if hearing the sea. Skylight windows

are tight shut slabs of opaque glass, precious stones in a crown;
and climbing onto the weave of vine, I am walking into coolness,

within the dimension beneath heat, colour stopped
on the cathedral roof of the slope of the leaf.

Light is thrown by the curve over-arm, but inside, under stacked
multiples of oval, I sit in filtered light, a flushed

yellow saturating the limits of my sight. Redbrick oven wall
scalds under bare-soft feet, legs dangling

and an ant the size of a small dog ponders past then a gale,
breeze at any other scale, begins for a second unsettling the sun.

The leaves open again. I am too small to do them any harm.

Topology

I dream you in your sun-watered garden,
a route to us years now gone,
then walking through the trees to the lake
and my immersion in you and the light
on the water like you

and how we are made by the turns of the earth.
Still you are as steady as clay
and I shrink to you, in each step,
each lengthened moment of our meeting
stretches, until, unnamable

after no time I am without time
back in the stream of us
walking through our city, which watches,
then melts to new substance;
remember the girl's cry as she ran too close to the edge?

And yet the river slides on and I cannot stop its push,
unfathomable, unlit,
                    into the flux of us,
                                completed,
                                continuous.

The Bird Men of the Far Hill

Out on the hill wearing black like light,
carrying torches they cross the ridge
into the valley's flicker and break,
into spasm of flashes,
triggering moon into darkness.

They are watching the river's pendulous hook
against the rust of the landmass,
hoping for endings and clods
of soil to fall sharp
into the felt of the sea.
They are out on the hill, predatory.
They carry heavy stones in their pockets;
cold against their legs,
and are looking for strangers,
unknowns, tornadoes,
in the back of next door's shed,
in the glimpse of your eye.

They gabble, scribe hieroglyphs into the mud
by the golf course, to break open your breath,
seal you within their cages. Feathered bodies
swell at the thought of your quietness.
They want to flatten your thighs.
They want to emit all their hurt.
They want you to take them
until you are as barren
as the winter ground
or as pock-marked as the muddy field.

*

The mulch you find yourself in
is sticky, wet,
filtered mountain, tree bark, excrement.

You are made into slope,

turfed over, never found,
speaking only out of the roots of newly-seeded grass;
the football pitch
studded with boot-marks.

You speak into the dusk
       but unheard, now detritus,
            the river drags your remains,
          you're soil; you crumble

out into the reaches of the estuary.
Spawning salmon swim over your smallness,
fish scales and meaty hulks
            groaning against your
                    dispersal
into salt and sea-vacuum,
        dark depth,

        alteration.

Seal Skin

Sun shifts through the clouds' broken shade.
A red fox flits like a bee.
She runs as fast as the east wind blows
from the motorway to the sea.

In the house at the edge of town,
her family keeps within
a girl's shape in a leaded jar,
the memory of her skin.

> Her body forms from shifting sun,
> cloud water becomes a lake.
> As she runs like wild earth turns,
> leaves from the spring bud ache.

And she runs without her skin;
a glimpse from a passing train,
a shimmering ghost in fading dawn
through the bracken by the lane.

She pounds the frantic carriageway
like a hunted deer
weaves amongst the cut of cars
yet only he can see her.

> Her body forms from shifting sun,
> cloud water becomes a lake.
> As she runs like wild earth turns,
> leaves from the spring bud ache.

And he knows where this will end,
turns the key in the car engine lock;
glances again, breathes in and out,
the horizon in his look.

And she runs like the wind is full
in the sails of a tilting boat,
calling to the land as she goes,
New buds make me a coat.

And calling to the land as she runs
Clouds give me your grey faces
like a sky before the thunder
sticks to my open spaces.

And calling to the land as she runs
Soil in the tractor's furrow,
give me your warm damp earth
your grainy dark tomorrows.

A field rises like a swarm of flies,
till drenched in mineral-brown,
throws dry earth over her bare shoulder.
she is strata like a mountain.

> Her body forms from shifting sun,
> cloud water becomes a lake.
> As she runs like wild earth turns,
> leaves from the spring bud ache.

He turns the car into the single track
which leads towards the gate.
A no-entry sign swings in the rain.
A gull perches, quietly waits.

In the oil-seed crop she runs like time
and on through the silent yard.
Fattened pigs all kept in lines,
hens held in sound-proofed barns.

He stands on the muddy track
as she comes, mesh of leaf and soil,
rain heavy as the ocean floor,
her belly bulbous as a seal.

And blubbery and flecked with grey
his skin a soft furry sheen.
He holds her in his arms and sighs,
You run like you can swim.

Across flat fields pours the sky,
sea escaped from a bulging coast,
culverts swell till they burst like stars
and the two seals are submerged.

Their bodies shift with changing tides
and strong-born waves begin.
They swim like wild earth dives
as salt crystals encrust new skin.

The Cruel Mother

after the ballad

Amongst the leaves I lie
teeth-bared,

raw as the sundown.
Scattered skins hang on the trees

like prayer flags – I am demon,
I am the bad-one.

I am the wild, edible bark.
You bit my tongue and made me roar.

I will barren you, bust up your eye,
scratch at damp dirt with these claws.

Where are you? Nest of twigs,
den in the woods,

hut with smoke at the door.
The home burns its riches.

My young slide onto the forest floor like eels.
They writhe –

branches hold them. Swaddle
small forms with dirt. They call

on into the blistering night.
Sky bubbles and caws.

Trees like dogs lick at the sun,
wide as horizon, large as moon.

The oak I lean on leans back,
bark like a spine.

Over the fence on the well-kept lawn

I hear them talk –

O there is nothing to be done,
nothing, nothing to be done.

And hear him say
It is not his fault.

And they all agree
it was all up to me.

In the green wood
I sing to hope of rain.

I sing to blood
which falls and pours;

in the garden they sit, drink wine
and thunder, wonder

where I have travelled towards
but don't stand and search

but talk, and worse they sigh,
O there is nothing, nothing to be done.

I will eat these babies,
cook them one by one.

The green wood says I should stay the night.
The green wood casts a curse

on those who say nothing can be done
and leave me, a wild cat, to run

into their sleep in hot damp beds,
into their eyes in the dark.

I am a clawed mother
and he will not have them back.

O the cruelty he weighed on me.

Blue Black

...*coming ashore in the wilds of the Wirral,*
whose wayward people both God and good men
have quite given up on...

       Gawain and the Green Knight
       trans. Simon Armitage

The Norsemen left them in their well-nailed ships,
The sad survivors of the darts, on Dingesmere
Over the deep sea back they went to Dublin.

       The Battle of Brunanburh

Yr wylan deg ar lanw, dioer
Unlliw ag eiry neu wenlloer,
Dilwch yw dy degwch di,
Darn fel haul, dyrnfol heli.
Ysgafn ar don eigion wyd,
Esgudfalch edn bysgodfwyd.
Yngo'r aud wrth yr angor
Lawlaw â mi, lili môr.
Llythr unwaith, llathr ei annwyd,
Lleian ym mrig llanw môr wyd.

Truly, fair seagull on the tide,
the colour of snow or the white moon,
your beauty is without blemish,
fragment like the sun, gauntlet of the salt.
You are light on the ocean wave,
swift, proud, fish-eating bird.
There you'd go by the anchor
hand in hand with me, sea lily.

       The Seagull
       Dafydd ap Gwilym, trans. Hopwood

Before this I was a gull.

I flew from the city
        over the blue-black estuary, along the shoreline
                towards the abandoned lighthouse.
I flew through the wind-farm's rotating blades.
I flew over the river's rain-battered sheen,
        sodium spots lined up into a pattern
                of a peninsula's edge, fairground-lit,
        houses strung along the coast like lanterns,
        a black-railed prom stretching to distant
                        heavy mountains, marshland and flat fields
                backing away from the sea wall, grazing cattle,
a long tarmacked path through trees
        to the beach and submerged forest
                offshore, deep in sand,
        shimmering white transparent woods vatic in the waves

and with my gull's eyes I watch from above,
        from up here, on the air currents;
                the children are two black dots
                running over the shingle from the dark night's sea
                towards a woman on her knees
                in the moonlit sand, wide-opened arms
        as if she is holding a towel on a summer's day
                though it is a December's night. Is she me?
I look through her eyes to focus on the children.
        A girl, a boy, naked, about six and three:
                faces fuzzy around the edges,
                        with hair and eyes but no definition,
                they just keep running over the wet sand,
        sea rough behind, outline of a container ship on the horizon.

I try to fly inland towards the ridge
        but air currents push me back towards the edge.

I am kneeling, arms outstretched, squinting into darkness,
small pale bodies running towards me.

I am hovering over the shoreline, over the estuary,
children running over wet sand, a woman on her knees,

then she's walking to dry land, shingle in her boots.
I follow her return towards glass-sharp dunes.

And she drives, her hands fixed on the wheel,
two empty seats in the back of the car,
shadow splashed on ripped upholstery,
seat-belts swinging, turning to the lights,
a three-eyed wolf at the edge of the track,
and the road ahead wet and sandy,
pitted with last week's storm.
An easterly catches and I am among flooded fields,
webbed feet tacked onto moulding wood
as the vehicle rolls out of view
to the cross-roads by the motorway.

I'm flung north,
each wing stretched into darkness
above a house with one light in the top floor window,
and there she is parking in the driveway,
closing metal gates on the semis across the street,
opening the front door, curtains full on cold glass.

I can see her unpacking a bag on a table, turning
on a radio, staring out of the gap
in brocade straight at me
here in the blue-blackening edges of the sky,
suited to this rain that starts again
and up and away
behind her, behind me into the curve of the land
about a mile beyond her home, car, fence,
and further out at sea

tide turns, a stone wall rises
        from beneath green swell, marks out
            a harbour wall, long smothered
        by salt, where a ship is moored,
    unloaded, a clinker low on fine water, well-nailed
        steam-bent oak and pegs, a carved
                dragon's head on its prow;
    voluminous sea subsides to sand
            then marsh, then earth, brown-furrowed mud
        and chariot-tracks, mastheads clutter distance,
        a barge steadies on the tidal flow.
Sunlight blasts the scene with coppery emulsion.

She closes floral curtains; waves filter detritus.
Drowned plastic bottles sink into coarse sand.

    We are with her in empty rooms
    and fossilised nights.
    We are with her on blank blue
    afternoons of silence and repeat,

        sings marram grass to the wind,
            blowing dunes into back gardens,
    flicking shingle scratches onto conservatory windows,
        catching feathers which turn me around
            and over the shore. In the shallows
                two children still play,
            throwing sand at each other's eyes.

The night is an owl, round-faced and poised. It hunts
            mice in the rapeseed crop
        behind rows of pebble-dashed houses,
    sliding doors level to a new-laid patio.
She is eating at the kitchen table,
        spoon into bowl, to mouth to spoon to bowl
            and return; behind the extension

in an upstairs bedroom, mauve curtains wide,
        a man rocks between the legs of a red-haired woman,
his hands on her wrists, she laughs.
They put out the light.

As the moon slots itself back into the jigsaw sky
    I am over fields again,
        pulled towards sea's rolling dark;
  and at the shoreline's square corner,
      deep under high tide,
          prom abruptly halted on the beyond,
           a small island and mountains,
      waxy waters weave amongst red sandstone
of eroded land licked off into suspension;
        water bubbling, iron-bitter,
each return rubs sand onto sand
    and rocks beneath water's hold
        stratify into auburn folds on fold:
erosion precise, waves expand
    spaces, small fish
        turn within sudden shallows,
           flicker tender silver bellies to the moon;
    and I am upon them, reaching hard
        into cold wet spray, shimmer,
        rip, salted blood and sweetness.

Wind fastens itself to slippery land.
A car on the coast road coils towards the marsh.

A fish shines out at sea.
I survey and flinch, a creature far away,
        a seal strayed from the island's shadow side.
But looking sharp I see two children
        swimming a gentle breast-stroke
           through black water, as if in a pool.
           Serious-faced in parallel they dive and flip,

small feet flicking into air like tails,
and emerge several breaths away
towards the horizon-line and endless dark.

From the gatepost I see her running,
car stopped suddenly on the verge, door flung open,
running, long hair static in wind,
running across the beach. Her feet
drown in dry heaps, until on wet sand
she is running towards the sea, her face
flushed pink, blood rough
deep in her chest cavity, an inland sea
sweats in folds of her jumper, sweat on her thighs,
running to the dark, to the blue-black,
and on the horizon the seals tip into and out
of flow, are standing on the platform
of the ocean and waving finned hands,
flags in the wind.

I spear the night, under-sung
in the battle of the blue-black
straining towards dawn,
as globule rain, teal-coloured, fog-soaked,
is a heavy oily liquid spooling
like tide into rock-pools
and the night takes me up again
over the bay and into the sky,
over the marsh around the small town
where on a promontory a tall man stands helmet-proud,
alert to fresh dark, his hair
limp with wetness, street-lights before him,
a succession of animals' eyes.
He picks up an oar, wades through the shallows
as I am thrown up and over the marina,
over white dinghies moored in the harbour.

Three men process carrying a torch;
it marks them out atop the cliff.
    Moving slow, a convoy across a plain, past the estate house,
        corn field, sugar beet crop, sandstone church,
        they press on along back roads tarmacked quiet,
    rain thickening. I follow over mountainous roofs,
        skylights' warm yellow, aerials, a forest canopy.
Gables channel torrents
        as the three men are striding along the ridge now,
            eastwards along the well-walked route.
                Their reflections shine against
                a fluorescent poster in the chip-shop window,
                    late night offie just locked up,
            owner smoking a ciggy as he turns the corner
                away from their procession.
The men stop and look,
                        an unexpected wall, a new-build,
            navigate the underground reservoir,
                stored waves churning beneath thin grass,
            pattern edges of the playing fields,
                sail the allotments
                    to the A-road again, not stopping
                    to look, just on through the gate to the small hill
                        bright with sun. Red daylight streams
                    from among trimmed hedges as other men
                            also helmet-proud step out
            all inland now. Water holds north, east and west.
At a window a girl watches the men speaking in the field.
Her mother closes pink curtains
                and she shivers pressed beneath sharp sheets,
motorway's throb a distant heartbeat
        and I am almost asleep,
                turning through grains of dust
                    which trail my flight across the peninsula

to the crematorium by the roundabout.
It still glows raw and red.
    I see a man leaning on a gate,
        small knife in his hand. It glints
        as I leave him to his darkness.
            He is raging into the blue-black.

In the brook diverted beside the railway, muddy
        but swollen with excess rain, two
    children bob along, heads held high, clamber onto the bank,
        sit and let their legs dangle into depths,
            stare straight ahead, then dive.

At the corner of the out-of-town car park
        she pulls up, runs, pushes through a hedge,
            but the children have sunk back into mud.
I can see their outline from above.
They are giggling, lying like flat fish beneath the stream
        and over towards the woods, on the ridge,
            past unknown bones in breeze-block stables,
                over horses, one leg bent, stone-still,
pegged across the slope, a dark dun pony in a blue
        blanket eyes my flight across cloudless, end-paper sky.

On the line of the hill
        a cry strikes. On the mulch, blood stains
            into leaves; a man's body in shadows
            slashed hard, slumps into bone in seconds.

I rise above the hill, this red hill, green fields
    below dotted with men in battle, fighting hand to hand
        with spear and shield. They are

        battling amongst the telegraph poles
        battling amongst the ploughed earth
        battling amongst the tractors, parked in the farmyard.

Each man blooded; an inland sea.
Each body dissolves to soil when it hits the furrows
　　　　until the field is emptied of flesh
　　　　　　but runs red, sharp scarlet;
　　　　　　　　a yellowed autumn day
　　　　and a young man feeds hay into a harvester,
　　　　then gone, just darkness and threat of dawn.
Blue-black weight is the night,
　　　　seals redness into brown earth
　　　　　　waterlogged with too much rain.
Field a fen; crop rotten,
　　　　　　and through blood-clogged dirt
　　　　　　two children run as if into the sea on a summer's day,
　　　　　　　　laughing, hair streaming scarlet, mahogany
　　　　　　　　　　drenched skin. They seem to revel in it.
　　　　　　　　　　A car howls away towards the coast.

And the ships on the river sail for the north.
And the barge on the river sails for the south.
And the sun in the east sails for the west.

She drives below me,
　　　　her eyes fixed on the road.
Wipers tic as she waits at the lights.
　　　　In a front room of a pebble-dashed house,
　　　　　　one stray lamp on, a woman
　　　　　　　　stands by net curtains
　　　　watching more rain and a passing car.
　　　　　　She holds a model ship,
　　　　　　　　she rips apart slowly,
　　　　　　tearing thin cotton from the rig and the mast.

And I swoop away over our ink-written shore, swooning
　　　　through full wetness
　　　　　　and double back. I loop, I cry

at all movement, gaping sea
hurrying towards me.
I crash in, diving beneath the rough of the flow.
Within folds, blackness slips
and swims. Hunger-driven,
but not rewarded I float
beyond the island as wooden ships
are leaving. Sailors
heave oars into cut sea as I dive again,
returning, fishless, but coiling north
around plinths of turbines
the boats navigate like sandbanks. Being opaque,
the crew need no light, cannot
be seen on radar or from the tanker
churning its way into the wide estuary mouth,
though the long-ships' glimmer,
on the local ferry's glossy hide.
And from the ocean I can see her
take the marked track across massed dunes.
Mascara in her eyes, she wears a thin coat,
keeps moving through the dark terrain
to a turning towards the beach,
watching felt night, listening to my call,
following high tide and a bold moon;
and on the north shore, from the lighthouse
she is running to the blue-black,
then kneeling, arms outstretched
as if on a summer's day
for two children bobbing on the tide.

Gulls in the storm,
gulls on this tide,
beaks wide open to catch her breast,
she lets open to the rain.

Notes and Acknowledgments

'Tide' in *Poetry Wales* (Winter 12-13 Vol. 48 No. 3)

'Dusk Town' commissioned by *Time to Read* for a reading at Runcorn Central Library, October, 2012. Also published in 'The Lighthouse Literary Journal' *Gatehouse Press*, London, (October 2014)

'A Burial of Sight', commissioned for conference on Arts and Health, FACT, 2009 and first published in a pamphlet of the same name by *The Word Hoard*, Todmorden, 2012. Also published in *Dark Mountain Anthology* (2012)

'Arne's Progress', created and published as an broadside newspaper in collaboration with illustrator, Desdemona McCannon, (Arne Press, 2012)

'Crossing Over' and 'Mainline Rail' in *The White Review*, (2013)

'In My Ears and In My Eyes', an internet collaboration with Adam Steiner for 'Camarade, Enemies in the North', (*Cornerhouse*, Manchester, March 2013. Also published online in *The Clearing* (September 2013)

'Topology' in *Vield the Pole*, (February 2014)

'Seal Skin' and 'The Cruel Mother' written in conversation with folk singer, Emily Portman.

'Blue Black', quotation from 'Gawain and the Green Knight', trans. Simon Armitage, (Faber, 2009). 'The Battle of Barunburth', *A Choice of Anglo Saxon Verse*, Trans, R.A.Harmer (Faber, 1970). 'The Seagull', Dafydd ap Gwilym, Trans. Hopwood, *Singing in Chains*, Listening to Welsh Verse, Mererid Hopwood, (Gomer Press, Ceredigion, Wales, 2005)

With many thanks to the University of Exeter and the AHRC for supporting my practice-based PhD research and thesis '"Making Connections": The Work of the Local Poet'. Thanks to all the poets, artists and musicians whose generosity and energy is invaluable, and to friends and family for all your support. Thanks also to Andy Brown, Deryn Rees-Jones and Dave Ward for their editorial advice and feedback.